How To Use This Study Guide

This five-lesson study guide corresponds to *"Rick Renner Answers Your Difficult Questions" With Rick Renner* (Renner TV). Each lesson in this study guide covers a topic that is addressed during the program series, with questions and references supplied to draw you deeper into your own private study of the Scriptures on this subject.

To derive the most benefit from this study guide, consider the following:

First, watch or listen to the program prior to working through the corresponding lesson in this guide. (Programs can also be viewed at **renner.org** by clicking on the Media/Archives links or on our Renner Ministries YouTube channel.)

Second, take the time to look up the scriptures included in each lesson. Prayerfully consider their application to your own life.

Third, use a journal or notebook to make note of your answers to each lesson's Study Questions and Practical Application challenges.

Fourth, invest specific time in prayer and in the Word of God to consult with the Holy Spirit. Write down the scriptures or insights He reveals to you.

Finally, take action! Whatever the Lord tells you to do according to His Word, do it.

For added insights on this subject, it is recommended that you obtain Rick Renner's books *Last-Days Survival Guide*, *No Room for Compromise*, *Dressed To Kill*, and *You Can Get Over It*. You may also select from Rick's other available resources by placing your order at **renner.org** or by calling 1-800-742-5593.

LESSON 1

TOPIC
The End Times

SCRIPTURES
No scriptures were shown on the TV program.

GREEK WORDS
No Greek words were shown on the TV program.

SYNOPSIS
The five lessons in this study, ***Rick Renner Answers Your Difficult Questions***, will focus on the following topics:

- End-Times Questions
- 'How Do I Get Started in Ministry?' and Difficult Local-Church Questions
- Random Doctrinal Questions
- Questions About Finances With an Emphasis on Giving
- Questions About Relationships and Conflicts

The emphasis of this lesson:

In this lesson, Rick answers your end-time questions concerning the rapture of the Church and reveals what he believes is the single biggest challenge facing the Church today. He also shares the trending direction of society as well as what will likely happen in the Church in the coming years.

When we look around today, it seems as if the whole world has been turned upside down in its thinking. Wrong is called right, and right is called wrong. Chaos and confusion seem to abound as deception runs wild — even within the Church. We are living in the last of the last days, and here are the answers to some of your questions concerning the end.

A Note From Rick Renner

I am on a personal quest to see a "revival of the Bible" so people can establish their lives on a firm foundation that will stand strong and endure the test as end-time storm winds begin to intensify.

In order to experience a revival of the Bible in your personal life, it is important to take time each day to read, receive, and apply its truths to your life. James tells us that if we will continue in the perfect law of liberty — refusing to be forgetful hearers, but determined to be doers — we will be blessed in our ways. As you watch or listen to the programs in this series and work through this corresponding study guide, I trust you will search the Scriptures and allow the Holy Spirit to help you hear something new from God's Word that applies specifically to your life. I encourage you to be a doer of the Word He reveals to you. Whatever the cost, I assure you — it will be worth it.

> Thy words were found, and I did eat them;
> and thy word was unto me the joy and rejoicing of mine heart:
> for I am called by thy name, O Lord God of hosts.
> — Jeremiah 15:16

Your brother and friend in Jesus Christ,

Rick Renner

Unless otherwise indicated, all scripture quotations are taken from the *King James Version* of the Bible.

Scriptures marked as (*GNT*) are taken from the **Good News Translation - Second Edition** © 1992 by American Bible Society. Used by permission.

Scripture quotations marked (*MSG*) are taken from *The Message*, copyright © 1993, 2002, 2018 by Eugene H. Peterson. Used by permission of NavPress. All rights reserved. Represented by Tyndale House Publishers, Inc.

Scripture quotations marked (*NIV*) are taken from The Holy Bible, New International Version® NIV®
Copyright © 1973, 1978, 1984, 2011 by Biblica, Inc.
Used with permission. All rights reserved worldwide.

Scripture quotations marked (*NKJV*) are taken from the *New King James Version*®. Copyright © 1982 by Thomas Nelson. Used by permission. All rights reserved.

Rick Renner Answers Your Difficult Questions

Copyright © 2022 by Rick Renner
1814 W. Tacoma St.
Broken Arrow, OK 74012

Published by Rick Renner Ministries
www.renner.org

ISBN 13: 978-1-6675-0263-2

eBook ISBN 13: 978-1-6675-0264-9

All rights reserved. No portion of this book may be reproduced or transmitted in any form or by any means — electronic, mechanical, photocopy, recording, scanning, or other — except for brief quotations in critical reviews or articles, without the prior written permission of the Publisher.

QUESTION 1: Why do you believe so strongly in the Rapture?

When it comes to the topic of the Rapture, the Church today is quite divided. Surprisingly, only a small percentage of Christians believe in the rapture of the Church, and what's worse is that many don't believe in the Rapture at all. In fact, if you mention that you believe in the Rapture among some Christians, you will be laughed at, ridiculed, and even attacked.

This increasingly hostile response is actually a fulfillment of prophecy. The apostle Peter said, "…Scoffers will come in the last days, walking according to their own lusts, and saying, 'Where is the promise of His coming? For since the fathers fell asleep, all things continue as they were from the beginning of creation'" (2 Peter 3:3,4 *NKJV*). The fact that people — including some Christians — are questioning the Lord's return for His Church is clear evidence we are in the last of the last days.

Make no mistake — the rapture of the Church is plainly taught in Scripture, and one of the clearest passages that teaches this truth is First Thessalonians 4:15-18, where Paul wrote:

> **For this we say unto you by the word of the Lord, that we which are alive and remain unto the coming of the Lord shall not prevent them which are asleep.**
>
> **For the Lord himself shall descend from heaven with a shout, with the voice of the archangel, and with the trump of God: and the dead in Christ shall rise first:**
>
> **Then we which are alive and remain shall be caught up together with them in the clouds, to meet the Lord in the air: and so shall we ever be with the Lord.**
>
> **Wherefore comfort one another with these words.**

Notice Paul said that we which are alive and remain will be "caught up together" with the Lord in the clouds. The words "caught up" are a translation of the Greek word *harpadzo*, which means *to catch*, *seize*, or *take away*. It carries the idea of *snatching someone suddenly out of great danger*, just in the nick of time. Taking into account the Greek meaning, this passage states that the Lord Himself is going to descend from Heaven with a shout or mighty command that rallies together all of Heaven's army. The voice of the archangel will speak, the final war trumpet will sound, and then the lively remnant of believers who are actively living and looking for Jesus to come will be snatched suddenly from the earth and forever be with the Lord!

The Holy Spirit prompted the apostle Paul to also write about this amazing event in First Corinthians 15:51 and 52, which says:

> **Behold, I shew you a mystery; We shall not all sleep, but we shall all be changed, in a moment, in the twinkling of an eye, at the last trump: for the trumpet shall sound, and the dead shall be raised incorruptible, and we shall be changed.**

One of the reasons people struggle to understand the Rapture is because it is a *mystery* and not a subject a person can easily wrap their heads around. Nevertheless, it is a clear teaching of the Bible. "We will not all sleep" means not all believers are going to die. There will be one generation of living believers that will be changed "in a moment, in the twinkling of an eye." The Greek here literally says in *an atomic, indivisible moment of time,* our physical bodies will undergo a supernatural *metamorphosis,* and we will be gloriously changed!

Interestingly, there are numerous rapture-like occurrences all throughout Scripture. From the sudden disappearance of Enoch in Genesis 5:24 to the Rapture of Elijah in Second Kings 2:11 to the ascension of the two tribulation witnesses into Heaven in Revelation 11:12, the truth of the rapture is biblically sound.

For a verse-by-verse study on the rapture of the Church, we recommend that you obtain Rick Renner's series *The Coming of the Antichrist.*

QUESTION 2: What do you believe is the biggest challenge facing the Church today and in the next few years?

Rick said, "I believe the biggest challenge facing the modern church is the LGBTQ+ movement and transgenderism."

Indeed, pastors are going to have to deal with the fact that there are gay people in their churches who are going to claim that it's okay to be gay and love Jesus. As a matter of fact, some pastors are already being confronted by individuals making this claim, and if it hasn't come to your church yet, get ready, because it's on its way.

We're living in a world that is being modified rapidly by the spirit of the age. Sadly, because Christians don't know the teaching of the Bible, they don't know what God says about what is right and about what is wrong. The enemy has masterfully used culture and the media to make many believers think that if they take a stand against something, they're narrow-minded and bigoted. But the fact is, those who oppose homosexuality are just standing on the side of Scripture and agreeing with its distinction about what God says is wrong.

In addition to the LGBTQ+ movement, the idea of transgenderism is another major challenge pastors are going to have to really come to grips with. There are people in churches today who have children that are claiming to be a different gender than that which they were born. More and more hurting and confused individuals are being duped by the devil's deception that they are not the sex that they were born. Consequently, they are undergoing gender reassignment surgeries — all because their thinking has been modified to believe it is okay.

Like it or not, pastors are going to have to take a position on these issues. We can already see the three different camps that are forming. Some are taking the position of Scripture and agree that when God creates every human being, they are created male or female (*see* Genesis 1:27). They are either one or the other, and there's no gender fluidity. Then there are other pastors who may not agree with transgenderism or LGBTQ+, but because they don't want to be viewed as "judgmental" or "intolerant," they will be silent and accommodate the behavior. Still, other pastors will openly embrace these behaviors and join the chorus of the corrupt culture that celebrates it.

Clearly, these battlegrounds will be a major dividing line of the Church in the next decade.

As it stands now, the law is against those who stand by Scripture regarding these issues. It is possible that this may result in persecution, which shouldn't surprise us. Jesus said one of the telltale signs that the end of the age is near is that His followers would be persecuted (*see* Matthew 24:9). For many years, the Western church has not experienced much persecution like the Church in other parts of the world. But that has begun to change — even in America.

Society is demanding that everyone conform to the new perverted norms or face the consequences. As crazy as it seems, there are even some school boards that are offering books to their very young children that teach them to accept that they can change their gender. Situations like these have left parents scrambling for direction on what to do.

Remember, the number one sign Jesus said would mark the end of the age and His soon return was *rampant deception* in the world and in the Church. That's why He said, "…Take heed that no man deceive you" (Matthew 24:4). The word "deceive" here is the Greek word *planao*, which means *to morally lead off track*. This was the very word used by Rabbis to describe a time at the end of the age when demon spirits would be released into the earth that would create delusional thinking.

Over 2,700 years ago, Isaiah prophesied that a time of delusional thinking would come. He said, "Woe unto them that call evil good, and good evil; that put darkness for light, and light for darkness…" (Isaiah 5:20). Friend, that's the day in which we are living. Many in society are so deceived and confused they have become reprobate in their thinking.

Now, when we use the word *reprobate*, people often don't understand its meaning. In Greek, the word "reprobate" is the word *adokimos*, and it describes *a mind that was created to be brilliant in many aspects, but now something has happened to it*. It's been bombarded by lies and deception again and again and again, and now it's malfunctioning. It doesn't think the way it once did. Instead, it's been modified to think in a brand-new way, and what we find is that when you have reprobate thinking, you believe that what is wrong is right.

The fact is, when it comes to the issues of transgenderism and the gay movement, if you listen to the people who are endorsing it, they really believe what they're saying is right. Although they may be very sincere, their minds are ill-affected and they're thinking in a reprobate manner. Again, this confirms Jesus' teaching that at the end of the age deception is going to come to the whole world; it's going to be the age of reprobate or delusional thinking.

QUESTION 3: Where do you see society going in the soon-coming years?

Amazingly, God gave the apostle Paul supernatural vision to be able to see 2,000 years into the future and prophesy the condition of society in the last of the last days. In Second Thessalonians 2:3, he said, "Let no man deceive you by any means: for that day shall not come, except there come a falling away first...." For starters, we need to understand that the words "that day" refer to *the day of the Lord*. Thus, before the day of the Lord, there is going to be *a falling away*. The Greek word for "falling away" is *apostasia*, which describes *a worldwide mutiny or rebellion against God*. It is *a turning away from the Lord* and *a throwing off of the law and the old established ways of thinking* in order to embrace a new, progressive way of thinking — a woke perspective.

Without question, we are living in the fulfillment of this scripture! Once this worldwide mutiny has taken root in society, the world will be primed and prepared to receive the antichrist, who is also called "the lawless one." The Bible says, "...That man of sin [will] be revealed, the son of perdition; Who opposeth and exalteth himself above all that is called God, or that is worshipped; so that he as God sitteth in the temple of God, shewing himself that he is God" (2 Thessalonians 2:3,4).

The apostle Paul goes on to say, "Remember ye not, that, when I was yet with you, I told you these things? And now ye know what withholdeth that he might be revealed in his time" (2 Thessalonians 2:5,6). Apparently, something is keeping the antichrist from being revealed right now. We'll see what that is in a moment.

Paul continued, "For the mystery of lawlessness is already at work; only He who now restrains will do so until He is taken out of the way" (2 Thessalonians 2:7 *NKJV*). In the original Greek, the end of this verse says, *"until He be removed right out of the middle of everything."* Here, the apostle Paul is talking about the Church. As the Church, we are the temple of the Holy Spirit (*see* 1 Corinthians 3:16), and as long as we're on the earth, we are a restraining force that is holding back evil. Once the Church is removed, evil will rush in and fill the void. The removal of the Church is the Rapture, and that day is coming soon!

Immediately after the Church is raptured, the Bible says, "And then shall that Wicked be revealed, whom the Lord shall consume with the spirit of his mouth, and shall destroy with the brightness of his coming: Even him, whose coming is after the working of Satan with all power and signs and lying wonders, and with all deceivableness of unrighteousness in them that perish; because they received not the love of the truth, that they might be saved" (2 Thessalonians 2:8-10).

Did you catch the last part of that verse? Through Paul, the Holy Spirit said that there is going to be a great number of people that are offered the truth, but they will reject it. Second Thessalonians 2:11 says, "And for this cause God shall send them *strong delusion*, that they should believe a lie." Basically, because these people have rejected God's offer of salvation through Christ, God says, "Okay, have it your way. Since you don't want the truth, believe the lie." Interestingly, the words "strong delusion" in Greek would best be translated as *energized deception*. Those who willfully and repeatedly reject Jesus — the truth — will be ensnared by energized deception.

We are seeing the early signs of this happening in the world in the form of transgenderism and the LGBTQ+ philosophies. People are so deluded, that they are surgically modifying their bodies to match their deluded thinking. The Bible predicted this type of bizarre behavior thousands of years earlier. It is a vivid sign that we've come to the very end of the age.

For a verse-by-verse study on what will take place in society during the last days and how to protect yourself from being sucked into its warped thinking, we recommend that you obtain Rick Renner's book *Last-Days Survival Guide*.

QUESTION 4: What do you believe is going to happen in the Church?

In the midst of the worldwide moral meltdown we are experiencing, several things are already happening in the Church and will continue to happen as time progresses. Rick gives a vivid snapshot of what's shaping up in the Church in his book called *No Room for Compromise: Christ's Message to Today's Church*:

> It's no secret that the spiritual environment in the world is undergoing a radical change right now. Unfortunately, what we're currently seeing and feeling is only the beginning of the rift that's developing within the Church. Unless a major revival occurs, this rift will only grow deeper and wider, and if repentance doesn't melt the hearts of people throughout the church world, it will eventually seem like there are three churches.
>
> Church number one: a church that holds fast to the truth and faces the brunt of opposition because it refuses to bend. Church number two: a church in the middle trying to ride the fence through accommodation or compromise in order to avoid persecution and societal rejection. And church number three: a lukewarm, Laodicean-like church that has allowed compromise

to run its full course, stripping it completely of the power of God, and leaving Jesus standing on the outside.

Thus, there are going to be three kinds of churches that emerge at the end of the age — the age in which we are now living. The question you need to ask yourself and answer is which church are you going to be a member of? Make your choice wisely — your eternity depends on it.

QUESTION 5: Why do you use the *King James Version*?

Rick shared that the reason he uses the *King James Version* is because it's still the Bible that is most widely used. The fact is, every Bible version is a translation of the original text. That means one or more people are restating what the original Hebrew and Greek say. Although the Word of God is without error, there are errors sometimes in the translation. The *King James Version* is still a treasured favorite of many believers, including Rick, which is why he continues to use it.

QUESTION 6: Why don't you use your platforms to address political issues?

In answer to this question, Rick said, "I don't believe I'm called to do that. I think some people are called to address political issues, and to them, I say, 'Bravo!' If somebody feels called to use their public platform to address political issues, that is their right, and it takes real bravery to do so. But I know that for me, that is not my assignment. I know I'm not to go there, which is why you've never seen me talk about political issues. Now, I will take a stand on *moral* issues, which is what I've done in this lesson. That's the job of a preacher, which is what I am. If you feel the need to use your platforms to address political issues, go for it! Just remember to do it in the Spirit of Jesus."

STUDY QUESTIONS

> **Study to shew thyself approved unto God, a workman that needeth not to be ashamed, rightly dividing the word of truth.**
> **— 2 Timothy 2:15**

1. We as the Church are called to both stand for the truth and to love people the way Jesus loves them, but that doesn't mean it will always be easy or clear-cut. What guidelines does God give us to help us

understand what this looks like? (Consider Romans 12:18; Ephesians 4:15; First Peter 3:15; and John 13:35.)
2. According to Luke 17:28-30 (and Matthew 24:37-39), Jesus said that the last days would be like the days of who? What do you see in their stories that sounds like today? (Consider Genesis 6:1-22; 19:1-29.)
3. What does the Bible say about our gender, the value of our bodies, and how we should treat them? Read these verses for the answers and ask the Holy Spirit to make these truths real and relevant in your life.

- **Genesis 1:27,28; 2:24,25 and Matthew 19:4-6**
- **1 Corinthians 3:16,17 and 6:15-20**
- **Romans 12:1**
- **Ephesians 5:29**
- **1 Corinthians 7:9**

PRACTICAL APPLICATION

But be ye doers of the word, and not hearers only, deceiving your own selves.
—James 1:22

1. Who do you know personally who's been struggling with their gender/sexual identity? What else do you know about their story? Ask God to show you a way to pray for and reach out to them and show them His love in a way they need it.
2. Sexual sin can often be scrutinized and stigmatized by people in the Church to the point that many of us are afraid, confused, or frightened at the thought of trying to interact with someone who struggles with it. Does that describe you? How do you normally respond to a person who is struggling with sexual sin? How did Jesus treat people who were living in sexual sin? (*See* John 8:1-11.) Invite the Holy Spirit to show you how and empower you to treat people in the same way.

LESSON 2

TOPIC
'How Do I Get Started in Ministry?' and Difficult Local-Church Questions

SCRIPTURES
No scriptures were shown on the TV program.

GREEK WORDS
No Greek words were shown on the TV program.

SYNOPSIS
Being called into ministry is truly a privilege, but it is certainly not without its challenges. If you feel as though God has called you to get started in ministry, there are a few things you really need to know — including the fact that ministry is all about serving others. Indeed, the local church is a place to serve the Lord by serving others and watching them learn and grow. But what are you to do when conflicts arise? And is there ever a time when it's okay to leave a church God led you to? Get ready for more answers to your questions!

The emphasis of this lesson:

Rick shares his personal story of how he got started in ministry as a boy and how handling yourself and your responsibilities behind the scenes determines whether you can be trusted with bigger things. You'll also discover the right way and the right time to leave a church as well as the value of both the young and the old in the church working together.

QUESTION 1: 'How do I get started in ministry?'

The most important must-have for starting out in ministry is knowing that God has called you. Knowing you have been called serves as an anchor when the storms of life hit and attempt to blow you off course or shipwreck your faith. Here is what Rick shared in response to this question:

> I knew I was called to the ministry from the time I was a very young man. I just had a veracious love for the Bible and a mother who would sit by me regularly and read Scripture. She's in Heaven now, but I'm so thankful to her for all she invested in my life.
>
> Back in those days, we had vinyl records that played Bible stories, and I would listen to those records for hours and hours, just being thrilled by the teaching of Scripture. I was probably between the ages of five and eight years old, and God had already hooked my heart. So much so that I had already begun serving in the church.
>
> The first thing I did in ministry was to work with my daddy, who was the church janitor. Each Saturday, he would assign me one section of the church and pay me 25 cents to clean it. He would say, 'Ricky, I want you to go up there with this rag and water and keep rubbing all the scuff marks on the linoleum until you get rid of them.' There were so many scuff marks on those old floors I thought I would never get them off. Again and again, my dad would remind me, 'We want these floors to really shine, Ricky, because we are doing this for the Lord.'
>
> Time passed, and I began to sing in the choir as well as participate in Sunday school training union, which was a staple activity for all Southern Baptists. My family and I were always there for training union, and if there was visitation on Wednesday night or Saturday, we were there for that too. We were serving, serving, serving, which is what ministry is all about.

Some believers think that being called into ministry is like being hit with a bolt of lightning from Heaven. They believe that suddenly the glory of God is going to fall on them and usher them into ministry. For some reason, they believe they're going to instantly step onto the stage and begin teaching, but that's just not how God works. He tests us one step at a time. Honestly, it's to our benefit that He doesn't work the "instant" way, otherwise we would not be prepared for it. Rick continued:

> Years later, when I finally entered the university, I was really wanting to teach the Bible. I told the leaders of the church, 'Please

give me an opportunity to speak,' but in their wisdom, they made me wait. They wanted to know I would be faithful serving in more menial positions in the church, so they had me setting up chairs, washing coffee cups, and vacuuming the carpet, which was grungy and full of stains. Nevertheless, it was my job to make the carpet look good, so I scrubbed and scrubbed that carpet to make it look its best.

Regardless of the task they assigned, I used the time to pray in tongues. As I set up the chairs, I laid my hands on each one, praying for the people who would sit in them and asking God to give me a good attitude. 'Lord, You know what I really want to do is teach and preach,' I'd say. 'But if this is what I can do, I'm going to do it with all my heart.' Sure enough, the day finally came when I was asked to begin teaching publicly.

When Denise and I got married, we were serving in a big denominational church alongside a well-known pastor. Once again, I was assigned many menial jobs by the pastor that I really felt were beneath me. He had me raking his leaves, shining his shoes, and washing and vacuuming his car. Although I really despised it at the time, I know now that it was good for me. God used each humble task to test my motives and break pride out of my life.

Oftentimes we are told to do things we dislike and don't want to do because we think they're below us. It's during those times, however, that God is watching our attitude to see if we qualify for the next assignment. And guess what — those times of testing never end. We're always in a period of qualification. Even at my present stage in life, God is still testing me periodically, watching to see if my attitude is right.

If you're being asked to do things on your job or at your church that seem to be beneath you, you are likely being tested. God is watching to see if you are doing things with a humble, joyful attitude. Likewise, He's looking to see your level of faithfulness and willingness to do whatever you're asked. How you handle yourself and your responsibilities behind the scenes will determine whether you can be trusted with the privilege of serving people from center stage.

The fact is, this life is a qualification period to determine what we get to do in Heaven. We're not just going to sit on clouds and play harps all day — we're going to be assigned specific tasks and get to rule and reign with Jesus. If we don't do well *now*, we won't qualify for a preferred assignment *then*.

The apostle Paul talked about God's preparation process. In Second Corinthians 1:21, he said, "Now he which stablisheth us with you in Christ, and hath anointed us, is God." Notice what comes first in this verse: God *establishes* us and then anoints us. Most people want to receive God's anointing first, but before God anoints us, He tests us to make sure that we're faithful and firmly established in Him. Once He knows we're grounded in His Word and are producing the fruit of His character in our lives, He will release His anointing on us and through us.

The Bible reveals that Paul had received a great deal of revelation from Christ during the three years he was in the wilderness (*see* Galatians 1:15-18). But when he began his ministry, he served side-by-side with others as a leader in the church of Antioch for many years. Paul's apostolic ministry was not launched until God saw that he was established in Him and faithful in the position to which he had been called.

So if you want to begin in the ministry, be faithful where you are right now with everything you've been asked to do. Express to God your desire to do what you feel called to do but leave the timing of things in His hands. Although our tendency is to anxiously watch the clock and think that time is ticking away, God is not a clock watcher. He's a character watcher. He is watching to see if we have matured and are ready for the next step.

Take your eyes off the clock and put them on Jesus. As you're waiting for your ministry to begin, study His life and focus on doing what God has asked you to do — and do it with joy and excellence. If you do it with a good heart, it will qualify you to move forward into the next phase. Again, all ministry begins with serving and continues with serving.

QUESTION 2: 'What if I don't agree with the direction my church is headed?'

It is inevitable that at some point you will not agree with something your church has decided to do. Whether it's a church of 100 or 1,000 people, there will be differences of opinion. We are all different people with different convictions and different ideas. The more people there are, the more ideas and opinions there will be.

Nevertheless, there is only one head in the local church, and that head is the pastor. Think about your physical body. You have two eyes, two ears, two feet, and two hands with many fingers. But you only have one head, and it's your head that calls the shots. If your body limbs begin to function on their own, something is desperately wrong, and you would seek medical attention.

In the same way, Jesus is the Head of His Body — the Church (*see* Ephesians 1:22,23), and as the Head, He gives direction to us. To help Him oversee the Church, He has appointed a pastor to shepherd each local church. Pastors are equipped with spiritual eyes to see and spiritual ears to hear what God desires. Moreover, the pastor has the mouth to declare what God wants the church to do. It is the pastor who casts the vision of the church and sends signals to the entire body about where it is to go and how it's supposed to function.

We're God's people, and God is a God of covenant. When you join yourself to a church, it's more than just saying, "Oh, I attend this church." On the contrary, you become a member and you make a covenant with that pastor, the leaders, and the congregation. It is a commitment that is not meant to be taken lightly.

Unfortunately, when some believers in a church don't agree with where the church is headed, they quickly jump ship and change churches. Some Christians are constantly in disagreement with the pastor over them, and they change churches all the time. The sad thing is, if you look at their lives, they also often change jobs, friends, and even marriages in the same way. They've developed the habit of breaking covenants when things get hard.

When you come to a point of disagreement with your church, don't immediately leave. Instead, pray. Usually, if you'll just wait a little while and pray for God's wisdom and strength, the struggle in your soul will dissipate and disappear. The next time you don't agree with or like the direction your church is going, and you feel as though it has gotten off track, pray. If the church never gets back on track, then it may be time to pray and ask the Holy Spirit to lead you somewhere else.

QUESTION 3: 'How do I know when it's time for me to start going to another church?'

To help answer this question, consider this real-life example Rick shared. A very dear friend of his was attending a church for many years, and at some point, the church entered into error. They literally began going in an unscriptural (heretical) direction, and as a result, people began leaving left and right.

If the church you're connected with begins teaching heresy, either the church needs to change what it's teaching, or you need to change churches. Again, a decision of this nature should not be made haphazardly. When God calls you to a church, you need to be faithful to it for as long as you can.

However, when you come to a point where you feel like you're a round peg being forced into a square hole and you're consistently grieved by going to church, then it's time for you to pause and pray a prayer like this:

> *Lord, You see how this church and I no longer fit together. I'm going in one direction, and they're going in another. It's not the same church that it was when I joined it. I'm no longer a blessing to the pastor or the people, and I really don't want to be a faultfinder that's constantly complaining about what's going on. So, rather than me continuing to go to this church every week and be grieved about what's happening and have a bad attitude, I'm asking You to release me from here and lead me to another church where I can be a blessing and be in agreement with its vision. In Jesus' name. Amen.*

Keep in mind that no church is perfect. It doesn't matter what church you go to; you're going to have moments when you may think things are not being done completely right — and you may be right. The church may be off in what they're doing. Realize that everyone in that church is a human being — including the pastor — and he may have made a mistake. So extend mercy to the leaders and the people, and don't be in a rush to leave. Slow down, be patient, and take your grievance to God in prayer. If He nudges you to confront an issue, do so out of love for everyone involved.

If you sense God's release and peace to go to another church, take time to go to your current church leaders and say, "Thank you for all the time we've had together and for pouring into me and my family. I am very grateful for what God has taught us, but now we really believe it's time to move on." In your departure, don't burn bridges. Instead, always be available to pray for and help the leaders and congregation. Live free of offense.

QUESTION 4: 'What does the Bible say about the older and younger generations learning to work together, especially when it's so needed in these days? Two trends I have seen are: The younger generation of church leaders is getting rid of the older generation to appeal to a younger target market; and in contrast, many in the older generation are trying to keep their glory days going longer, and in doing so, they're unwilling to mentor the younger generation because the change for them is so uncomfortable.'

A great example from Scripture to help us answer this question is the story of when Rehoboam, Solomon's son, became king over Israel. At that time, Rehoboam still had some of his father's counselors to advise him on his decisions. They were the voices of older, seasoned leaders. At the same time, he also had the input of his closest friends, which were the younger generation that was emerging.

A careful study of First Kings 12:7 reveals that the counsel of the older generation was very solid advice. But the younger generation — those who had grown up with Rehoboam — didn't like it and they convinced Rehoboam to reject the elders' counsel and accept their advice instead, which is exactly what he did. Needless to say, what resulted was catastrophic.

Clearly, there is value in both the older and younger voices — *both are needed in the Church.*

If you're older, please don't discount yourself or think of yourself as "washed up" or "out to pasture." Believe that God has promised you a long life — as much as 120 years, just as He gave Moses (see Deuteronomy 34:7). If you're 60, you still have half your life to live! In fact, new scientific research shows that the brain starts working at its maximum between the years of 60 and 80! It's in this time frame that your mind begins to kick into high gear and work at peak performance, which is contrary to what most believe about dementia and other things they say cause a person to think slow and forget.

Rick is now in his mid-60s and finally feels he has something valuable to give to younger people. Never let others discredit your value or put you on a shelf because of your age. There are people all around you that need something you have.

Churches that just pander to the youth and ignore or ostracize the older believers are cutting themselves off from a wealth of wisdom. On the flip side, any church that rigidly holds on to the past and is closed to pouring into and training the next generation is overlooking a source of passion, energy, and new ideas that can keep the Gospel relevant and active in the midst of changing times.

For the Church to be truly effective, we need both the young and the old as well as those in between. We need to learn how to get along together and humbly accept input from each other so that we can do what God has called us to do. So, you who are younger, have respect for those older who've pioneered the road before you. And you who are older, respectfully embrace the younger ones who are coming up in the church and look for ways to guide and mentor them. This will serve to create a much healthier atmosphere of unity in the Church and invite God's blessings!

QUESTION 5: How do you dwell in the secret place of the Most High?

In Psalm 91:1 (*NKJV*), the Bible says, "He who dwells in the secret place of the Most High shall abide under the shadow of the Almighty." This is a very powerful verse that begins a long list of promises God made, but He didn't make them to everyone. This passage clearly tells us that only those who "dwell in the secret place of the Most High" are the ones who abide — or live — under the shadow of Almighty God.

Dwelling in the secret place means *staying very close to the Lord*. Think about this: Let's say you were walking with a loving family member who was taller and stronger than you. In order to walk in his or her shadow, you would have to walk together and stay very close to them. The same is true about walking in the shadow of God.

Therefore, the promises God makes in Psalm 91 are made to those who are walking very near to Him. Anyone who is living in known sin is away from God and cannot lay claim to these promises. So learn to deal with the issues quickly and willingly in your life and walk close to the Lord. When He moves, you move with Him. Where He stays, you stay. As you stay in step with Him and abide in His shadow, all the promises of Psalm 91 belong to you.

QUESTION 6: What is the fullness of time referred to in Galatians 4:4?

In Galatians 4:4, the Bible says, "When the fulness of the time was come, God sent forth his Son, made of a woman, made under the law." In this passage, the "fullness of time" refers to the period in history from the time Alexander the Great and Emperor Hadrian were in power.

Alexander the Great was the leader of Greece that conquered the Medio-Persian Empire and who successfully spread the Greek language around the world. For the first time since the tower of Babel, the modern civilized world all spoke one language, and as a result, everyone would be able to hear the Gospel.

Hadrian was the emperor who built roads that connected the whole Roman Empire. His construction projects served to make a way for Gospel preachers to travel anywhere for the first time ever. In that moment of time, when everyone in the Roman Empire could speak the same language (Greek) and they were connected by roads, Jesus came.

STUDY QUESTIONS

Study to shew thyself approved unto God, a workman that needeth not to be ashamed, rightly dividing the word of truth.
— 2 Timothy 2:15

1. What does Jesus say about dealing with conflict in the Church and correcting each other as believers? (Take a look at Matthew 7:1-5 and 18:15-19.)
2. According to these scriptures, how can you recognize when someone is genuinely a false teacher? And what are the signs that someone is genuinely being led by the Holy Spirit — as a leader or otherwise? (Consider First John 4:1-3; Matthew 7:15-20; Galatians 5:22,23; and James 3:13-18.)
3. Take some time to carefully reflect on Psalm 91 and describe what life looks like when we "dwell in the secret place of the Most High, under the shadow of the Almighty."

PRACTICAL APPLICATION

> **But be ye doers of the word, and not hearers only,
> deceiving your own selves.**
> —James 1:22

1. Have you ever found yourself wondering whether you should stay in a certain church or under a specific leader? What did you do? Looking back, do you now wish you had done something differently? If so, what would you tell your past self? If not, what's a piece of advice you learned that you would give someone else in the same situation?
2. It can be easy for us to have a lopsided, generational approach when it comes to life and ministry. Do you find yourself leaning more toward a traditional, *older* way of thinking or a more out-of-the-box, *younger* mindset?
3. Why do you think you lean that way? Who do you find yourself at odds with as a result? Ask God to show you how to discern and be open to hearing from Him through someone you have tended to see as "too old" or "too young."

LESSON 3

TOPIC
Random Doctrinal Questions

SCRIPTURES
No scriptures were shown on the TV program.

GREEK WORDS
No Greek words were shown on the TV program.

SYNOPSIS
The answers to life's questions are found within the pages of Scripture, which is why the Holy Spirit prompted Paul to say, "Study to shew thyself approved unto God, a workman that needeth not to be ashamed, rightly

dividing the word of truth" (2 Timothy 2:15). There is no other book on the planet like the Bible! When you read it, it reads you! Although it is sometimes difficult to understand, Jesus has gifted us with pastors and teachers to help decipher what is being said — which is especially helpful when it comes to understanding key doctrinal issues.

The emphasis of this lesson:

In this lesson, Rick unpacks the meaning of Ephesians 4:26,27, how Jesus manifests when two or more of us are gathered in His Name, and why Jesus sent the legion of demons into the pigs. You'll also discover what it means to truly forgive someone, the reason there are four gospels, and what happened to Mary the mother of Jesus after His crucifixion.

QUESTION 1: Do all the promises God spoke to Israel apply to believers today?

No, they do not. There are some promises that God spoke directly to Israel and Israel alone. First Corinthians 10:32 helps answer how God speaks to us. It says, "Give none offence, neither to the Jews, nor to the Gentiles, nor to the church of God." In this passage, the apostle Paul mentions three groups of people that are on the earth, all of which can be placed into one of three groups: *Jews*, *Gentiles*, and *the Church of God*.

First of all, there are Jews, which are the descendants of Abraham, also known as the nation of Israel. Then there are Gentiles, which are all the non-Jewish, unsaved people of the world. And lastly, there are the people of God, which is the Church. A careful reading of Scripture reveals that God makes specific promises to each one of these groups.

- He makes promises to Israel that are only for Israel.
- He makes promises to unbelieving Gentiles about future judgment that just apply to them.
- And God makes promises to the Church that are solely for the Church.

Now while every promise made to Israel does not apply to us, the principle within the promise may apply. First Corinthians 10:6 confirms this saying, "Now these things were our examples...." Verse 11 reiterates, "Now all these things happened unto them for *examples*: and they are written for our admonition, upon whom the ends of the world are come."

So even though certain verses are not promises made to us — the Church — the principle, or main emphasis, of the promise is for us and can be applied to our lives.

QUESTION 2: I'd be grateful if you could shed some light on Ephesians 4:26.

Ephesians 4:26 and 27 says, "Be ye angry, and sin not: let not the sun go down upon your wrath: Neither give place to the devil." Some people read this and think that it's a sin to be angry, but that's not what the passage is saying. What it says is, "Be angry and sin not...," which means as believers, we should be angry about sin in our lives but have no tolerance for it. We are to use the anger over sin as a motivation not to give it an inch in our lives.

Verse 27 says, "Neither give place to the devil." The word "place" here is a form of the Greek word *topos*, which literally describes *geographic territory* and is where we get the word for a *topographical map*. This word *topos* lets us know that when we go to bed with a bad attitude, or if we're holding on to an offense or unforgiveness toward someone, it opens the door for the devil to attack us — especially in our mind and our emotions. It's as if we lease him a piece of land in our soul that he begins to occupy and use to increase his assaults against our minds. To be angry about sin and "sin not" means we put up a barrier and say, "I'm not going to go there; I'm not going to participate in that ungodly attitude."

When it comes to your relationships, you should never go to bed angry with anyone. Knowing this, if you find yourself angry at the end of the day, it would be good for you to take some time before going to sleep to say, "Lord, please forgive me for being angry with [person's name]; help me forgive them just as You've forgiven me. I don't want to go to bed with anger in my heart or open a door to the devil. I choose to forgive [person's name] and bless them as You've instructed us to do (*see* 1 Peter 3:8,9). In Jesus' name. Amen."

QUESTION 3: How does Jesus manifest Himself where two or three are gathered in His Name?

In Matthew 18:20, Jesus said, "For where two or three are gathered together in my name, there I am in the midst of them." It is important to note that Jesus didn't say, "For where two or three are gathered together *in the same room*, there I am...." With the advances in technology we have today, we can also be gathered together in Jesus' name via the internet, TV, or radio. Although we're not necessarily in one physical place, we can still gather together around a computer, cell phone, or television set with the purpose of praying, worshiping, and honoring Jesus.

How does Jesus manifest — or show up — in the midst of us? He shows up in the Person of the Holy Spirit. After Jesus died on the Cross and rose from the grave, He ascended into Heaven where He now sits at the right hand of the Father praying for us as our great High Priest (*see* Hebrews 7:25). In His place, He sent us His Holy Spirit to come and live inside of us *forever*. Jesus talks about the ministry of the Spirit in chapters 14,15, and 16 of the gospel of John.

Therefore, the time in which we are now living is the dispensation of the Spirit. God the Father and Jesus His Son are in Heaven. It is His Holy Spirit that is here in the earth and indwelling believers (*see* Galatians 4:6; John 14:17; 1 Corinthians 3:16). Hebrews 4:16 instructs us to come boldly before the throne of God in the name of Jesus and ask for His mercy and grace. So in those moments when two or more of us come together, Jesus manifests His presence through the Holy Spirit.

QUESTION 4: Why did Jesus send a legion of demons into the pigs?

The story of the demons being sent into the herd of pigs is found in three of the gospels, including Mark 5. As Jesus and His disciples made their way to the region of the Gadarenes, they encountered a man who was demonized like none they had seen before.

The instant this crazed man saw Jesus, he ran toward Him and threw himself down at His feet. Jesus immediately went to work bringing deliverance to him. The Bible says, "For he said unto him, Come out of the man, thou unclean spirit" (Mark 5:8). What's important to note in this verse is that the tense of the word "said" in Greek is ongoing. Hence, a better translation of this passage would be, "For Jesus kept on *saying* and *saying* and *saying* and *saying*, 'Come out of the man, thou unclean spirit.'" Another translation would be, "For Jesus kept on saying, 'Come out! Come out! Come out! Come out of the man, thou unclean spirit.'"

This lets us know that, initially, the demon spirits didn't budge, which was unusual because Jesus normally cast out demons quickly using a single word. When the evil spirits in this man wouldn't obey Jesus' repeated commands, Jesus asked, "…What is thy name? And he answered, saying, My name is Legion: for we are many" (Mark 5:9).

This explains why the demons were not easily coming out. This man didn't have just one demon — he had an infestation of demons. Specifically, he had a legion, which in Greek describes as *about 6,000*. As strange as it may seem, this man living among the tombs in a cemetery had about 6,000 demons living inside him! This demonstrates the enormous spiritual capacity of a single human being, which is much greater than most of us realize. If this man could house 6,000 demons, how much of God's Spirit can one person hold?

The truth is, we have more space for God in us than we've ever imagined. Our spiritual capacity is enormous, and we need to pray that we would be totally and completely filled with the Spirit of God.

When the demon answered and said, "My name is Legion," only one demon was speaking to Jesus. He was the elected spokesman for the rest of them. Mark 5:10 says, "And he besought him [Jesus] much that he would not send them away out of the country."

The word "besought" means *prayed*. The demon literally prayed to Jesus that He would not send them away out of the country. Verse 11 goes on to say, "Now there was there nigh unto the mountains a great herd of swine feeding." Keep in mind that this was the land of Israel, and the law clearly forbade the eating of pork. Therefore, pigs, which were unclean animals, should not have even been in the region

At this point, as Jesus kept repeatedly commanding and pressuring the demons to come out, the Bible says, "And *all the devils besought him*, saying, Send us into the swine, that we may enter into them" (Mark 5:12). Suddenly, instead of just one demon talking, all 6,000 devils started praying and begging Jesus to send them into the pigs. Can you imagine the volume and intensity of all those satanic voices?

The fact that these demons begged to go into the pigs demonstrates that evil spirits don't like to just roam in dry empty places. They want to indwell someone or something living. Demons will live in a dog, a cat, or in any other living organism they can occupy. Since this legion of devils wasn't going to be able to stay in the Gadarene man, they begged to be sent into the herd of pigs. Make no mistake: Pigs were low-level, filthy, dirty, and disgusting. The fact that the demons were willing to live in these low-level creatures shows how filthy, dirty, low-level, and disgusting they are.

In that moment, the Bible says, "...Jesus gave them leave. And the unclean spirits went out, and entered into the swine: and the herd ran violently down a steep place into the sea, (they were about two thousand) and were choked in the sea" (Mark 5:13). Interestingly, when you read this in the Greek text, it says the pigs were *being choked as they were running into the water*. As they were suddenly invaded and taken over by all these demons, the swine panicked.

The Bible does not say how long the man had that legion of demons lodged inside him. It may have been months or maybe even years. Whatever the case, the man remained alive — the demons could not take his life, even though they had tried to on several occasions (*see* Mark 5:5). Why? Because the man had a mind and will, and as long as a person has these, they have the ability to choose to resist the enemy, which is clearly what this man had done.

As bound as this man was, he was still in control of his mind. We know this to be true because the moment he saw Jesus, he ran to Him and began to worship Him (*see* Mark 5:6). The demons couldn't stop him because he exercised his willpower. The pigs, on the other hand, had no willpower, so when the demons came into them, they were immediately annihilated.

Jesus is letting us know that if demons had free rein to do whatever they wanted to do, they would kill, steal, and destroy everything they could. But they don't have free rein, and they are subject to the authority of Jesus Christ! In His Name, by His Word, and through His Blood, you, too, have supernatural authority over *all* the power of the enemy!

QUESTION 5: I've heard it said that if you forgive someone for a trespass, you also have to forget what that person did. Others say even though you must forgive someone who wronged you, you do *not* have to forget what that person did. What does Scripture say about this?

First, the word "forgive" is the Greek word *aphiemi*, which means *to release and to let go*. When you forgive someone for what they did, you just *let it go*. As a matter of fact, this word *aphiemi* (forgive) means to let it go *with no right to ever retrieve it again*. The use of this word indicates that when we forgive someone, we don't have the right to ever drag up that issue again.

That is exactly the way God treats us when He forgives us for our sins. Psalm 103:12 says, "As far as the east is from the west, so far hath God removed our transgressions from us." And in Jeremiah 31:34, God says, "…I will forgive their iniquity, and I will remember their sin no more."

This doesn't mean that God has amnesia. God is God, and He knows everything about everyone. But when He forgives our sins, they are cleansed from our life by the precious blood of Jesus, and under the Blood they remain (*see* 1 John 1:7,9). In His immeasurable mercy, God purposely chooses to "forgive" (*aphiemi*) and never to bring up our sins again. He lets them go and chooses to never retrieve them.

In the same way, we are told, "…Be ye kind one to another, tenderhearted, forgiving one another, even as God for Christ's sake hath forgiven you" (Ephesians 4:32). Now if someone has done something deeply hurtful to you, it will be very difficult to forget. Yet, while you don't have amnesia, you can make a decision to be like God and forgive the person and choose not to dwell on their actions anymore.

To be clear, forgiving someone doesn't mean we minimize what they did or that they are not accountable for their actions. It also doesn't mean that we stay in the same level of relationship with them. That would require reconciliation, which means they would need to sincerely apologize for how they wronged you and allow time for trust to be rebuilt. Forgiveness is a decision to let go of what they did so you can move on with your life.

If you ask Him, God will give you the grace to separate that person from their sin, as far as the east is from the west. That's what forgiveness is — it is a choice made by your will. There are no feelings involved. It is simply a decision of your will to let go of their offense and never drag it up again.

QUESTION 6: Why is the book of Ecclesiastes so negative?

Most often, this question is asked by younger individuals who haven't lived quite long enough to identify with what King Solomon wrote in his latter years. Indeed, the book of Ecclesiastes can certainly seem depressing, especially with repeated statements like, "Vanity, all is vanity."

But as we mature with age and acquire more life experiences, we come to better understand and even appreciate the book of Ecclesiastes. As we get older, our perspective on life changes, and we begin to realize that everything on this earth is indeed fleeting. By the time we come to the end of our life, we begin to see the big picture just as Solomon saw it and wrote about it at the end of Ecclesiastes:

> **Now all has been heard; here is the conclusion of the matter: Fear God and keep his commandments, for this is the duty of all mankind.**
> — Ecclesiastes 12:13 (*NIV*)

Solomon had absolutely everything a man could want, including big houses, extravagant clothing, the choicest foods, and more wealth and wisdom than could be measured. But when he came to the end of his life and he died, he couldn't take any of these things with him where he was going. Thus, learning to enjoy each moment of life as a gift from God and sharing it with those we love is very important.

So while the book of Ecclesiastes may seem extremely negative, it's actually just an assortment of common-sense sayings from a person who lived life to the fullest.

QUESTION 7: Why are there four gospels, and what is the difference between them?

Of the four gospels, three of them are very similar in the retelling of the life of Jesus Christ. These three are Matthew, Mark, and Luke, and they are called the *Synoptic Gospels*. They all tell the same story — each in a little different way.

Matthew's gospel was written for *Hebrew* readers — his audience was Jewish. Some scholars believe the gospel of Matthew is the only book of the New Testament that may have been written in Hebrew. We don't know that for sure, but some believe that.

Mark's gospel was written for *Roman* readers, and even though we call it the gospel of Mark, it is actually Peter's gospel. It was given the name "Mark" because it was physically penned by John Mark who served as Peter's secretary. Peter dictated the story, and Mark wrote it down.

Luke's gospel was written to *Greek* readers. In fact, in the New Testament, the writings of Luke and Paul had the best grammatical Greek.

So whatever story you study in one of the Synoptic gospels, you should study in all three, and then put all the details together to get the complete picture.

When you come to **John's gospel,** you will discover a unique masterpiece. It is the most theological of all the gospels, focusing on and proving the deity of Jesus. The Holy Spirit saw fit to move on all four of these individuals to write their remarkable versions of Christ's life because He knew we would need them all.

QUESTION 8: What happened to Mary after the crucifixion, and where did she die?

When Jesus was hanging on the Cross, pouring out His life for us, He had His mother, Mary, on His mind. Only one disciple was at the foot of the Cross at that crucial moment, and that was John — the one who called himself "the disciple whom Jesus loved." The Bible says:

> **Now there stood by the cross of Jesus his mother.... When Jesus therefore saw his mother, and the disciple standing by, whom he loved, he saith unto his mother, Woman, behold thy son! Then saith he to the disciple, Behold thy mother! And from that hour that disciple took her unto his own home.**
>
> **—John 19:25-27**

What's interesting to note is that 40 days after Jesus was raised back to life, Mary was present in the upper room with the 11 remaining disciples and the most devoted followers of Jesus (*see* Acts 1:13,14). When the Holy Spirit came to live in believers on the Day of Pentecost, Mary was there. She was one of the original Pentecostals. After that, she disappears from Scripture.

Yet we know from John's gospel that Mary was taken in by John himself, and he cared for her for the remainder of her life. Early Church history records that when John later moved to Ephesus, he took Mary with him, and she lived out the latter years of her life in Ephesus where she entertained and received apostles and church leaders. It was Mary herself who shared with Luke and the other gospel writers the stories about the nativity, Jesus' dedication day, and the time he got lost on their trip to Jerusalem. She had chronicled all those events in her heart and retold the details when the gospels were being written.

Today, there's a house on the hill above the city of Ephesus that you can visit, which is where Mary lived in the latter part of her life.

STUDY QUESTIONS

> **Study to shew thyself approved unto God, a workman that needeth not to be ashamed, rightly dividing the word of truth.**
> **— 2 Timothy 2:15**

1. What were the First Century believers doing when the Holy Spirit first came on the Day of Pentecost (*see* Acts 1:14; 2:1)? What did they continue doing (*see* Acts 2:42-47)? How are the promises of Psalm 133:1-3 related to the events that took place the day the Church was born?
2. Why do you think God wanted four different accounts of Jesus' story to be recorded in Scripture? Read the first and last verses of each gospel — what differences and similarities do you notice in their tone, purpose, and content?
3. Ecclesiastes is not the happiest book of the Bible, but there are several nuggets of wisdom throughout its pages that people of all ages — even the younger crowd — can benefit from. Look up these passages and take note of the sound, biblical advice God provides.

- **Ecclesiastes 3:1-8,11**
- **Ecclesiastes 2:24-26**
- **Ecclesiastes 4:9-12**
- **Ecclesiastes 10:10**

Like Jesus, we also represent the Father to those around us (*see* 2 Corinthians 5:20; 1 John 4:17). When it comes to dealing with demons and the spirit world, what gifts has God given you? (Consider Matthew 16:19; 18:18-20; Luke 9:1; 10:17-19; Second Corinthians 10:3-6; and Ephesians 6:11-18.) How does knowing what you have been given in Christ change your perspective on dealing with demons?

PRACTICAL APPLICATION

> **But be ye doers of the word, and not hearers only, deceiving your own selves.**
> **— James 1:22**

1. In this lesson, we learned that Jesus shows up in our midst in the Person of the Holy Spirit when we gather — physically or virtually

— with other believers. Can you recall a time when you sensed the overwhelming presence of the Holy Spirit? Where were you and what did you experience?

2. Do you want to experience more of the manifest presence of the Holy Spirit? Ask yourself:

   - How can I be more in sync and unified with believers around me?

   - What petty disagreements do I need to let go of?

   - Who around me needs to know I care about them, and that God loves them?

   - How can I make worshiping God more a part of my everyday life?

3. If someone were to ask you, "Who are you mad at?" who is the first person that comes to mind? Is there anyone else? Why are you angry with them? Have you noticed that anger affecting your life? If so, how?

4. We all have hurts that are hard to forgive, and sometimes with good reason. When we experience betrayal, neglect, or abuse, we often fear the same kind of injury again, so we build emotional walls and constantly remind ourselves of the past in hopes that we'll be safe from reliving it. What kind of pain are you most afraid of? The answer shows what — and who — you need to forgive. Invite the Holy Spirit into these areas and ask Him for the grace to truly forgive those who have hurt you and to heal the wound in your soul.

LESSON 4

TOPIC

Questions About Finances With an Emphasis on Giving

SCRIPTURES

No scriptures were shown on the TV program.

GREEK WORDS
No Greek words were shown on the TV program.

SYNOPSIS
One of the subjects Jesus talked about more than anything else is money. Actually, the Bible is filled with passages and stories about how we should and shouldn't handle our finances. What we do with the resources we've been given clearly reveals the allegiance of our heart. Indeed, "…Where your treasure is, there will your heart be also" (Matthew 6:21). The more we truly trust God as our Provider, the freer and more peaceful we will be in the area of our finances.

The emphasis of this lesson:

In this lesson, Rick meticulously explains the law of sowing and reaping found in Galatians 6:7 and shows how it applies to everything you give. You'll also learn what it means to "cast your bread upon the waters" and how to care for your seed once it's been planted. There is a "due season" to every seed you've planted, and you will reap a harvest if you don't give up.

QUESTION 1: After I asked God for financial provision and I'm waiting for it, what shall I do while I'm waiting?

To answer this question, let's look at some verses in Galatians 6. On the surface, reading this chapter seems to reveal contradictions in Scripture. For example, Galatians 6:2 says, "Bear ye one another's burdens, and so fulfil the law of Christ." The word "burdens" here is the Greek word *baros*, which depicts *a crushing, heavy weight*. It can refer to either *a physical problem, circumstantial problem*, or *spiritual problem*. In this verse, Paul is teaching us that when we see someone under a heavy load, rather than just look at them in pity and say, "What you're going through must be so difficult," we are to fulfill the law of Christ and crawl under their load with them and help them carry it.

What's interesting is that three verses later, Paul says, "For every man shall bear his own burden" (Galatians 6:5). Although this verse seems contradictory, it is not. The word "burden" here is the Greek word *phortidzo*, which describes *the backpack that was worn by every Roman soldier*. It was each soldier's responsibility to carry his own backpack; he couldn't ask anyone else to carry it for him. The parallel Paul is making here is that as individual believers, we need to carry what God has called us to carry. It is our responsibility — no one else's.

"What does this have to do with giving?" you ask. Well, in the context of this chapter of the Bible, which we'll see in a moment has much to say about giving, Paul is basically saying we each have our own responsibility to give what God has called us to give, and we can't expect someone else to do our part.

Galatians 6:7 is one of the most foundational teachings on giving in the New Testament. Writing under the inspiration of the Holy Spirit, the apostle Paul said: "Be not deceived; God is not mocked: for whatsoever a man soweth, that shall he also reap."

The word "deceived" in this verse describes someone who has bought the lie that giving is a scam and it doesn't work. Paul then added, "…God is not mocked…." This word "mocked" depicts *one who turns his nose up at God* as if to say, "I've heard this before, and it doesn't work. It may work for others, but it doesn't work for me."

When Paul said, "Be not deceived; God is not mocked," he is urging his readers not to buy the lie that giving doesn't work and not to turn our noses up at God in contempt. His rules or laws will not be violated. To help us grasp his point, Paul immediately gives a law in connection with giving: "…For *whatsoever* a man soweth, that shall he also reap" (Galatians 6:7)

Notice the word "whatsoever." It means *anything*. Whatever you sow — fill in the blank — that is what you are going to reap.

- If you sow **love**, then you're going to get *love* back.
- If you sow **patience**, then you're going to get *patience*.
- If you sow **forgiveness**, then when you need *forgiveness*, you'll receive it.
- If you sow **mercy**, then when you need *mercy*, you'll receive it.
- Likewise, if you sow **money**, you're going to get *money* back.

Something else that is very important here is the Greek tense of the word "soweth." It describes an ongoing action. Thus, it would better be translated, "Whatsoever a man sows and sows and sows and sows, etc." This is a *repeated* action, not something a person does once or occasionally. The sowing he or she is doing is a *habit* that is a part of his lifestyle. They are a *sower* — not just one who sows once or twice.

Equally important is the tense of the word "reap," which is also an ongoing action that agrees with the word "sow." Thus, we could translate this part of the verse, "Whatsoever a man sows and sows and sows and sows, (etc.), that shall he also reap and reap and reap and reap, etc." This lets us know that our level of reaping is determined by our level of sowing. If we are constantly sowing, we will constantly be reaping.

If you sow *once*, you're going to reap *once*. But if you sow *many* times, you're going to reap *many* times. To live in a cycle of reaping, you have to live in a cycle of giving, because your giving determines the level of your reaping.

The law of sowing and reaping applies to everything you give. Not only does this principle apply to how you give financially, but it also applies to how you treat people in your relationships. If someone has done you wrong, ask God for the grace to forgive them. One of these days you're going to need to be forgiven, and what you give the people who hurt you is what you're going to receive when you hurt others.

- If you give **kindness** to others, you'll receive *kindness* in return.
- If you give **time** and **attention**, you'll receive *time* and *attention* in return.
- If you give **help to those in need**, you'll receive *help* when you are in need.

Interestingly, many people in the world believe this principle, only they say, "What goes around comes around." Again, this is a general law that applies to everything including finances, but because it's a concept of sowing, which is agricultural, you have to think like a farmer.

A lesson from a farmer. When a farmer plants his seed, does he expect to come out and have a harvest the next day? Of course not: It takes time for a harvest to come. In the same way, when you plant your seed or financial gifts, you need to water them with prayer and watch over them, all the while listening to the Holy Spirit who will tell you how to nurture what you've planted. This nurture involves watering, removing the weeds that are trying to choke the plant, and chasing away all the pests that are trying to destroy it.

Rick told a story about how he decided to grow corn on a little piece of available land that was next to his daddy's garage. After going out and planting his corn seeds in a nice, neat row, he began to water them. Then he watched and waited intently to see them pop up through the soil. But as time dragged on and on and nothing was happening, Rick became so disgusted with waiting that one day he went out, took a spatula from the kitchen, and started digging up the seeds to see if anything was happening. When he dug up the seeds and saw that they had little sprouts on them, he thought, *Oh Lord, what have I done? I've destroyed my seed because I've ripped them out of the soil.*

In the same way, that's what we as believers sometimes do when we give to God and don't see immediate results. It is no wonder the apostle Paul said, "Let us not be weary in well doing: for in due season we shall reap, if we faint not" (Galatians 6:9).

There is a "due season" to every seed that you have ever planted, and God is the only one who determines that due season. Your job is to sow your seeds — which includes your finances — then watch over them and care for them by pulling the *weeds* out of your heart. Weeds are the cares of this life and offenses that tend to choke the life out of us. Next, you need to chase away all the pests, which represent the spiritual opposition that comes against you, and spend regular time in the Son-light of God's presence. If you ask Him, God will create the optimal environment to make your seeds grow, and in due season, you will reap a harvest if you don't give up.

What it means to "cast your bread upon the water." There are many Christians who have often quoted a passage in Ecclesiastes 11 about giving. Prosperity preachers have preached about it, pastors have taught on it, and congregations have even sung songs about it, but they often don't know what it means. The Bible says, "Cast thy bread upon the waters: for thou shalt find it after many days" (Ecclesiastes 11:1).

To understand this verse, we have to be familiar with where the writer took the illustration. When Solomon wrote this passage, he drew from the time when the children of Israel were living in Egypt, and part of their job was to grow wheat. History reveals that they would travel up the Nile River to where it was flowing, and they would throw their seed into the waters. The current would carry their seed downstream to the Delta Nile, which was marshy, and over time the seed would begin to take root and grow. Eventually, months later, the Israelites would harvest grain down in the Delta Nile, far from where they sowed their seed.

In the same way, we give our money into the Kingdom of God, and it takes time for it to get to where it's supposed to be to begin to take root and produce a harvest. If we don't "cast our bread on the waters" in faith and let the current of the Holy Spirit take our seed where it needs to be, it will never produce a harvest.

Something else is very important in Ecclesiastes 11:2. It says, "Give a portion to seven, and also to eight; for thou knowest not what evil shall be upon the earth." Although this may sound strange, it is basically telling us to diversify our giving and never stop giving. You may be living in a good time right now, but you don't know what economic challenges are coming. If you're constantly giving while you have the opportunity, planting your financial seed is a guarantee that no matter what happens on the earth, you're going to have what you need. God Himself is going to be taking care of you.

Ecclesiastes 11:3 goes on to say, "If the clouds be full of rain, they empty themselves upon the earth...." Here Solomon states a scientific fact: Clouds that are loaded with moisture produce rain that pours on the earth. That's basic science. The second part of verse 3 says, "...And if the tree fall toward the south, or toward the north, in the place where the tree falleth, there it shall be." Again, Solomon is pointing to a scientific fact — the law of gravity.

Essentially, he is asking the question, "Is the law of gravity ever denied?" The answer is no. And just as clouds full of rain always empty themselves and gravity is never denied, the law of giving is never denied either! When you cast your seed into the water, it's eventually going to produce a harvest. "...For whatsoever a man soweth, that shall he also reap" (Galatians 6:7).

QUESTION 2: Could there be instances where spiritual hindrances are holding back God's provision? What do I do in that situation?

Rick tells a story in his book *Dressed To Kill*, about a time when he and Denise came to an inexplicable moment when they had no money. Suddenly, and for no apparent reason, the offerings to the ministry slowed to a halt and the resources just dried up. It left Rick totally bewildered and greatly frustrated.

In an effort to stretch what little substance they had, he pulled out his calculator and began to crunch the numbers of the bills in front of him. But regardless of how he punched in the numbers, they just couldn't get out of the red. There was no light at the end of the tunnel and no feasible way to fix the major financial deficit in which they found themselves.

Day in and day out, Rick found himself praying about money and their desperate need for more of it. Some people have said it's really bad to be rich because all rich people do is think about money. But it seems even worse to be poor because poor people are in greater bondage to the lender. When rich people think about money, they're usually wondering where to invest it. But when the poor think about money, they never stop thinking about how much they need and how they can get more.

Rick became more and more desperate and his cries to God more intense. "Lord! How am I going to pay my bills?" he shouted. It seemed like every time he lifted his voice to Heaven and prayed, the word money was on his lips. "Money! Money! Money! God, we need money — *now!*" You would have thought *Money* was God's name because it was all Rick talked to Him about.

Then one day the Lord spoke to Rick and said, "You don't have a money problem, Rick."

"We don't?" he said sarcastically. "It sure looks like a money problem to me. If we don't have a money problem, then what kind of problem do we have?"

The Lord responded, "You don't have a money problem. You have a *spiritual* problem." And then He led Rick to Mark 4 and the story of when Jesus and the disciples faced a fierce windstorm at sea. Just hours before Jesus would cast the legion of demons out of the man of Gadara, the enemy tried to stop Him from reaching His destination. God showed Rick that it was spiritual forces coming against him trying to financially devastate the ministry.

In that pivotal moment, Rick learned there are times when spiritual winds of opposition try to stop us from entering the promise that God made to us, and we have to take authority over them in the name of Jesus. That is exactly what he and Denise did, and it's what you need to do too.

When Rick finally got his eyes off the calculator and addressed the spiritual force that was resisting them, it left, and within a short time, the financial flow into the ministry was restored to normal.

QUESTION 3: I've been extending my faith for God's provision in the area of finances. I know Rick Renner is not a financial expert, but with him having big dreams and starting at ground zero, could he comment on what the New Testament teaches about giving and finances?

When God asks you to step out in faith and do something for Him, He doesn't look at your bank account first to see if you have enough in it. Likewise, neither should you. If God has spoken something to your heart — and you know that word is from Him — you don't need to focus on money. Focus on the word from Him.

Obedience to what God has told you to do is like a magnet that attracts His power. If you'll just obey what God has told you to do, your obedience will attract the money you need like a magnet attracts metal.

Now that doesn't mean you don't take time to stop and count the cost of doing what He's asked (*see* Luke 14:28-31). God has given you a mind and He wants you to use it. There is also nothing wrong with seeking wise counsel before stepping out in obedience to what God has asked (*see* Proverbs 11:14). But the bottom line is, you can't let your own logical reasoning, or the opinions of others, carry more weight than what God has spoken to you. If you know what He's said, you need to step out in obedience — that's what God responds to.

Think about when God told Joshua to lead the nation of Israel into the Promised Land. Before they could do anything, they first had to cross the Jordan River, which was at flood stage. It wasn't until Joshua stepped into the Jordan with the priests that the waters parted. The same is true for you. If you will say yes to the Lord and step out in faith, when you put your foot forward in obedience, the waters of impossibilities will move! And your faith will attract the resources you need to get the job done.

QUESTION 4: What is the *RIV*?

The *RIV* is the *Renner Interpretive Version* of the Bible. It is not a translation because the *Renner Interpretive Version* is not a word-for-word translation. It is a conceptual interpretation.

Rick's training is in understanding classical Greek and deciphering the original Greek words that are used in the New Testament. Through diligent study, he mines out all the various meanings of the words in Scripture and then pulls them into the text to create a conceptual translation. The result is a version that provides a fuller understanding of what is really being communicated in each passage.

As wonderful as the *King James Version* is, it doesn't fully convey the rich depth of meaning found in the original Greek text. The *RIV — Renner Interpretive Version* — is designed to unearth the hidden gems of truth that we would otherwise miss while reading the majority of today's Bible versions.

Since the emphasis of this lesson is on finances, here is an example of a familiar verse of Scripture pertaining to finances. Philippians 4:19 in the *King James Version* says, "But my God shall supply all your need according to his riches in glory by Christ Jesus."

Taking into account the Greek meaning of the key words, here is the *Renner Interpretive Version (RIV)* of Philippians 4:19:

> **But my God will supply your needs so completely that He will eliminate all your deficiencies. He will meet all your physical and tangible needs until you're so full you have no more capacity to hold anything else. He will supply all your needs until you're totally filled, packed full, and overflowing to the point of bursting at the seams and spilling over.**

This promise was originally made to the Philippian believers who had sacrificially given to the spreading of the Gospel through Paul's ministry. It is a promise specifically made to people who were givers. Thus, this verse cannot be claimed by just anyone. Only those people who are faithful givers can claim this promise. If you're a giver who regularly sows your finances into God's work and where He directs you, you can confidently stand on and lay claim to Philippians 4:19.

STUDY QUESTIONS

Study to shew thyself approved unto God, a workman that needeth not to be ashamed, rightly dividing the word of truth.
— 2 Timothy 2:15

1. Severe financial lack can easily be one of the most emotionally debilitating challenges we'll experience in this life. Yet, God guarantees us again and again and again that He will take care of us! Look up these powerful promises in a few different versions of the Bible and write out the translation of each verse that best instills encouragement and hope in your heart.

   - **Psalm 34:9,10**
   - **Psalm 84:11**
   - **2 Corinthians 9:8**
   - **Philippians 4:19**
   - **Hebrews 13:5**

2. Even Jesus and His disciples found themselves in need of finances, food, and material provisions. How did God provide for them in each of these separate situations? What do these examples say to you personally about God's faithfulness?

   - **Matthew 14:13-21**
   - **Matthew 15:32-39**
   - **Matthew 17:24-27**
   - **Luke 8:1-3**
   - **Luke 22:7-13**

3. Giving is so close to God's heart that it's mentioned all over the Bible. What other instructions and promises does He give? Take a look at these additional verses and write out what the Lord reveals to you.

   - **Malachi 3:8-11**
   - **Matthew 6:1-4**
   - **Luke 6:38 and Proverbs 11:25**
   - **Proverbs 18:16**
   - **Proverbs 19:17; 22:9; 28:27**

PRACTICAL APPLICATION

> **But be ye doers of the word, and not hearers only, deceiving your own selves.**
> **—James 1:22**

1. How does knowing the historical context of Ecclesiastes 11:1 broaden your understanding of it? Is there a certain amount of "bread" God has been nudging you to give? If so, how much? And to what group or individual is He prompting you to give?

2. "Casting your bread upon the waters" can certainly feel scary and uncertain, especially when we have no earthly, visible guarantee of a harvest. This is true both of giving monetarily and in making consistent, godly choices over the long haul. What have you been most afraid to give? Time? Love? Forgiveness? Vulnerability? A commitment to purity? Pray and ask the Holy Spirit to baptize you with His boldness and to reveal and uproot the fear that's been holding you back.

3. Take a few moments to look at your answers to the previous two questions. What connection do you see between them? Invite the Holy Spirit to heal your heart of past disappointments and empower you to begin to give again. Even if it's just a little at a time, the habit of giving will grow stronger and stronger, and it will eventually fill your life with abundant fruit!

LESSON 5

TOPIC

Questions About Relationships and Conflicts

SCRIPTURES

No scriptures were shown on the TV program.

GREEK WORDS
No Greek words were shown on the TV program.

SYNOPSIS
Next to trust, being able to work through strife and forgive others is one of the most important elements of building and maintaining healthy relationships. God's Word says, "Out of respect for Christ, be courteously reverent to one another," and "Welcome with open arms fellow believers who don't see things the way you do…" (Ephesians 5:21 and Romans 14:1 *MSG*). The fact is, there will always be people who don't see things the same way you do. Each of us has our own ideas and our own opinions. Thus, experiencing conflict is inevitable. So, what is the right way to handle disagreements? Let's see what the Bible has to say.

The emphasis of this lesson:

As much as it is within your power, God wants you to live at peace with everyone. To achieve peace in your relationships, you're going to have to hunt for it. It isn't going to automatically come to you. When strife raises its ugly head in your relationships, deal with it because strife undealt with is a door opener for the devil to begin bringing deception and destruction into your life.

QUESTION 1: What does the Bible say about conflict?

Conflict is an inevitable part of life. Any time you have two or more people in a relationship, you have different opinions, which are sometimes very strong. One verse that is very important for cultivating healthy relationships is Romans 12:18. It says, "If it be possible, as much as lieth in you, live peaceably with all men." The phrase "if it be possible" in Greek really means *if it's doable*. Sometimes having peace with certain people is not doable. Nevertheless, if it is doable, as much as it is within your power, God wants us to be at peace with everyone.

Another verse that is very helpful when it comes to relationships is Hebrews 12:14, which says, "Follow peace with all men, and holiness, without which no man shall see the Lord." The word "follow" is a translation of the Greek word *dioko*, which is a hunting term that depicts *a hunter who is following the tracks of an animal*. He's decked out in his hunting clothes and has all his special gear as he methodically tracks down his game, looking for every sign and sniffing for every scent of the animal he's trying to catch. The Greek tense of the word "follow" indicates that he's *following* and *following* and *following* and *following*.

In our case, God wants us to "follow peace," which means if we want peace in our relationships, we're going to have to hunt for it. Peace isn't going to just automatically come to us. We're going to have to look for and follow the trail of peace. If we are not tracking down peace with others, and holiness, the Bible says we shall not "see the Lord."

Some have read this and thought that if they had bad relationships, they wouldn't go to Heaven, but that is not what it means. Understanding the meaning of the word "see" reveals what the writer is trying to tell us. The word "see" here means *to be admitted into the immediate presence of God*. So basically, this means if we have strife in a relationship, that strife is a blockade stopping us from experiencing the presence of the Lord.

Have you ever been in a church meeting where everyone around you is being blessed? They're weeping and rejoicing as the Holy Spirit is ministering to them, and you feel nothing? If you've wondered why that was the case, it was because you had strife in your life, and it was blocking you from a close connection with God.

Here is the example Rick shared from his life:

> When we first moved to the former Soviet Union, our family settled in the Republic of Latvia, and we lived in Riga, which is where we started our church. Before long, we went on TV, and God began miraculously blessing our efforts. But there was another pastor in town who wasn't very happy about it. The reason he wasn't happy was because he believed he was leading a new generation of believers into the future, and he felt that the whole city belonged to him. 'This city belongs to me,' he said, 'and I'm not sharing it with anybody.' Carrying great offense, he began to publicly cut me down and derail me.
>
> Well, I have to be honest and admit I didn't like him either. He was a little short guy, and he taught doctrine that I considered to be unbiblical. For example, he taught that every Christian was infested with demons, and consequently, they needed to be delivered again and again and again every week. I personally attended some of his services, and I watched as people vomited into boxes,

thinking they were delivering themselves of demons. They just worked themselves into a frenzy until they started vomiting.

These are Christians, I thought to myself. *They don't have demons.* It was doctrinal teaching like this, and his belief that he was the only one who could have a big church in Riga, that caused me to greatly dislike him. He even went so far as to publicly denounce me in one of his services, saying to his congregation:

'Well, there's another preacher in town who says God is going to use him to start a church. But let me tell you what I think of that preacher. He's bald, and anybody that's bald at that young stage in life is surely under some kind of a curse from God.'

When I heard what that little preacher told his church, I laughed. I started losing my hair very early in life and have been bald since I was about 17 years old. Having hair didn't mean much to me. But the more I thought about his cutting remarks, the more and more frustrated I became. Then one day, I found myself doing the unthinkable.

As I stood in my pulpit, I turned to our new church family that was growing very rapidly and said, 'I hear there's another preacher in town who says anybody who's bald is under a curse of God. Well, if you want to know what I think, I think anyone whose growth is stunted is the one who's obviously under a curse of God.' Honestly, I couldn't believe what I had said.

Sadly, my feelings toward this preacher became so bad that I began calling him the pigmy pastor. It seems with each passing week, my attitude grew worse and worse. Then one day when I was praying, the Lord said to me, 'Rick, do you want revival?'

'Oh, yes Lord,' I said. 'It's why I'm here.'

He said, 'Rick, I'm going to ask you again: Do you really want revival?'

Again, I answered, 'Lord, You know I want revival!'

He then asked me a third time, 'Do you really want revival, Rick?'

I said, 'Yes, Lord. I really want revival,' and I heard the Holy Spirit say, 'Then here's what you have to do: You need to get in your car, drive across town, and have a meeting with that pastor. You need to get on your knees in front of him and ask for his forgiveness for your attitude because it's your attitude that's blocking revival.'

'What about *him*?' I immediately snarled back. 'What about *his* attitude?' And the Lord said, 'I'm not talking to you about him. I'm talking to *you* about *you*.'

God was calling me on the carpet for my bad attitude, and I couldn't deny how bad it was. I'm sorry to say it took me about two months to obey what God told me. Nevertheless, the day finally came when I worked up the nerve to get in my car, drive to his church, and meet with him in his office.

Still dreading what God had told me to do, I began to beat around the bush, making small talk about the weather, our kids, and a bunch of other things that were unimportant. When there was nothing else to talk about, I said, 'Well, I need to tell you the real reason I'm here. I'm here to deal with me.'

I slipped onto one knee, and I thought, *One knee. That's as low as I'm going.* And the Holy Spirit said, 'Both knees.'

Reluctantly, I dropped down onto my second knee, and as I looked up to speak to him, he was leaning over his desk looking down at me. His eyes — wide-open with glee — seem to say, '*I can't believe it! Rick Renner is bowing before me!*'

Seeing him in that posture was so painful, I had to close my eyes. I reminded myself, *Rick, you're not here to deal with him; you're here to deal with you.*

When my mouth opened, I heard myself begin to ask for forgiveness, but it was in the wrong way. 'You know, you've done a lot of wrong things....' Again, I reminded myself, *You're not here to deal with him, Rick. You're here to deal with you.* I continued.

'But despite all of that, I'm wrong. I've talked about you, and I've said bad things about you. And I'm here today to ask you to forgive me.'

I can't tell you how much I wanted *him* to get on his knees and ask for forgiveness from *me*, but he didn't do that. Again, I reminded myself, *I am not here to deal with him; I am here to deal with me.* When I had finished sincerely apologizing and asking for forgiveness, I got up from the ground and I was free. From that moment forward, I put on my hunting gear and decided to hunt after and capture peace with that man.

My wife, Denise, and I invited him and his wife to our home for dinner, and we began to do things with them regularly. Today, many years later, that man and I are still very dear and cherished friends, and though we don't see each other often, we really appreciate one another. That's the power of following peace with all men.

Sometimes the best thing you can do to follow peace is to heed the timeless advice of Ecclesiastes 3. It says that there is "…a time to keep silence, and a time to speak" (v. 7) and "…a time to embrace, and a time to refrain from embracing" (v. 5). If you're dealing with a difficult relationship, you need to know when to talk and when to be quiet. Likewise, you need to know when to embrace and when to refrain from embracing and give somebody space.

Oftentimes those you are closest to are the most difficult to be at peace with. Your spouse, your kids, and your extended family can become like sandpaper in your life. Even siblings often have a hard time getting along. Nevertheless, God wants us to find a way to live at peace with them.

The good news is, the Holy Spirit is a master hunter who knows how to find peace in every relationship. As you learn to humble yourself and surrender to Him and depend on Him for wisdom in interacting with others, He will show you what to say and when to say it. He will help you restrain your tongue and not just say what comes to your mind. Your part is daily submitting to the Lordship of Jesus and obeying what He tells you to do.

For additional insights on this subject, it is recommended that you obtain Rick's book *You Can Get Over It* as well as his autobiography *Unlikely: Our Faith-Filled Journey to the Ends of the Earth*.

QUESTION 2: Jesus taught in Matthew 7 that we are not to judge lest we be judged. How, then, do we judge the fruit of a believer's life and yet

not fall on the fine line of improper judgment? I'm learning to discern between the two, and it would be really helpful to have a teaching on it.

To answer this question, we need to identify what Jesus is talking about here. When He says, "Judge not, that ye be not judged" (Matthew 7:1), He is commanding us not to be *judgmental* of others. The fact is, we live every day of our lives judging the things around us, and there's nothing wrong with that. We judge what is healthy and unhealthy to eat as well as what is a wise and unwise way to spend our time and money. Likewise, we judge whether someone is lying or telling the truth and whether a relationship is good or detrimental for us. Judging — or assessing — people, places, and things is just a natural part of life.

However, being *judgmental* of others is different. When Jesus says, "Judge not…," He is literally saying, "Don't live your life being critical, condemning, disapproving, faultfinding, or nit-picking of others." Being judgmental is a mindset where you lock into an opinion about someone that you can't break free of. It is often based on *prejudice*, which is a *pre*-judging of a person that is wrong and ungodly.

Unfortunately, many people misuse Jesus' words to build a wall of defense that keeps others from ever speaking a word of correction to them, which is not right. Out of genuine love and concern, we are told to speak the truth in love to one another (see Ephesians 4:15), and this will often include words of correction. The truth is, pride and fear often blind us from seeing and assessing things accurately in our own lives. We need people around us who will help us see our blind spots and address issues that we can't see — and they need us to provide the same insight into their life.

Again, judgment is just a part of life. It is discerning and assessing good from bad, right from wrong, and truth from error on all levels. Being judgmental is what we need to avoid and stay away from.

QUESTION 3: What happened between Paul and Barnabas that causes them to divide from each other?

When Saul, who we know became Paul, met Jesus on the road to Damascus, he was gloriously saved. But many of the believers in the Early Church — including the disciples in Jerusalem — were afraid of him and didn't believe his conversion was real. When the Hellenists plotted to kill

Paul, the apostles put him on a ship and sent him back to his homeland of Tarsus.

It was Barnabas who went to Tarsus and found Saul and brought him to the church in Antioch to help teach and disciple the large influx of new believers. At that moment, Barnabas was the spiritual leader in the relationship. He was the one who introduced Paul to the church leaders and helped reinstate him into the ministry. You might say Barnabas was like Paul's elder spiritual brother, and in those early years, Paul likely looked to Barnabas for counsel, support, and encouragement.

The Bible tells us that Paul's companion on his first missionary journey was Barnabas. Together, they pioneered uncharted territory, bringing the Gospel to places like Lystra, Derbe, and the island of Cyprus. As the years went by, Paul's anointing grew stronger and stronger and eventually eclipsed the anointing of Barnabas. Ironically, the person who was the leader was no longer the leader.

As Paul and Barnabas prepared to leave on their second trip, a major rift took place. The Bible says, "And some days after Paul said unto Barnabas, Let us go again and visit our brethren in every city where we have preached the word of the Lord, and see how they do. And Barnabas determined to take with them John, whose surname was Mark. But Paul thought not good to take him with them, who departed from them from Pamphylia, and went not with them to the work" (Acts 15:36-38).

John Mark, the person Barnabas wanted to take on the second missionary journey, was his sister Mary's son. Early Church history tells us that this Mary owned a big house in Jerusalem — it was the same house where Jesus' last supper was held and where Pentecost took place. It later became the meeting place for many church gatherings, such as the prayer meeting that saw the successful release of Peter from prison (*see* Acts 12:12).

Paul didn't want to take John Mark with them again because he had abandoned them on their first trip and returned home when things got tough. In Paul's eyes, John Mark was like an apple picked too soon — he just wasn't ready for such intense ministry. Nevertheless, Barnabas — John Mark's uncle — really wanted him to go, and the Bible tells us:

> **And the contention was so sharp between them, that they departed asunder one from the other: and so Barnabas took Mark, and sailed unto Cyprus; And Paul chose Silas, and**

departed, being recommended by the brethren unto the grace of God.

— Acts 15:39,40

Notice it says that "contention was so sharp between them." The word "contention" is the Greek word *paroxusmos*, which is a compound of the words *para* and *xusomos*. The word *para* means *to be alongside* and is where we get the word for a *parasite*; and *xusomos* is a word that means *to poke with a stick or sharpened instrument*. The use of this word *paroxusmos* — translated here as "contention" — means Paul and Barnabas were literally side by side exchanging sharp words — poking, jabbing, and verbally attacking each other.

And the contention became so sharp between them that they separated themselves from each other. Barnabas took John Mark and sailed off to Cyprus, and Paul took Silas and went through Syria and Cilicia. As far as we know, the two of them never ministered together again. From that moment forward, the apostle Paul remained active throughout the book of Acts, but Barnabas disappears from the pages.

Sometimes that's what strife in relationships will cause you to do — disappear. God just doesn't work through those who are in strife. Any ministry, marriage, business, or family that desires to stay in the anointing and blessings of the Holy Spirit should adopt a *no strife policy*. When strife raises its ugly head in your relationships, deal with it. Strife is a door opener for the devil to begin bringing deception and destruction into our lives (*see* James 3:16).

That's what happened to Barnabas and Saul — strife crept in between them and dissolved their relationship because it wasn't dealt with properly.

QUESTION 4: What is your personal favorite book of the Bible?

Rick shared that of all 66 books of the Bible, the book of Psalms has ministered to him over and over and over again. "I literally feed my soul on the book of Psalms," he said. "I read it nearly every morning. When I get up, I turn on the coffee pot, feed the dogs, grab my Bible, and go to a place where I begin to feed my heart the Word of God."

The book of Psalms is so impactful that when Rick finishes reading it, he starts all over again. It is a regular part of his spiritual regimen, and he repeatedly reads and meditates on the psalms because they provide strength, healing, encouragement, and hope. We encourage you to spend some time in the book of Psalms.

STUDY QUESTIONS

Study to shew thyself approved unto God, a workman that needeth not to be ashamed, rightly dividing the word of truth.
— 2 Timothy 2:15

1. What does God say again and again in Psalm 34:14; Romans 14:19; Second Timothy 2:22-24; Hebrews 12:14; and First Peter 3:11? Why do you think He repeats this instruction so frequently?
2. Without question, *strife is deadly*. Depending on the Bible version you're reading, strife goes by several names including *contention*, *rivalry*, *selfish ambition*, as well as *self-interest* and *selfishness*. According to Proverbs 13:10, what is the biggest cause of strife? Why is this so dangerous to you as a believer, and what is the only cure for this evil? (*See* Proverbs 8:13; 11:2; 16:18; James 3:16; First Peter 5:5.)
3. When Jesus said, "Judge not, that ye be not judged" (Matthew 7:1), He was telling us not to live our lives being critical, condemning, disapproving, faultfinding, or nit-picking of others. How do First Corinthians 4:5 and Romans 14:10-14 expand the reasons for not being judgmental of others?
4. Carefully reflect on Jesus' words in John 13:12-17 and the words of the apostle Paul in Philippians 2:3-8; Romans 12:3; and First Corinthians 10:24. What is the recurring theme in these passages? What do they speak to you personally that helps you stay out of pride and strife?

PRACTICAL APPLICATION

But be ye doers of the word, and not hearers only, deceiving your own selves.
—James 1:22

1. The Bible says, "Do everything possible on your part to live in peace with everybody" (Romans 12:18 *GNT*). Who in your life do you find it hard to be at peace with? It's possible that God is trying to use them to show you something about *you* that He wants to change. Pray

and ask the Holy Spirit to give you eyes to see this person the way He sees them and to learn what He wants you to know about yourself.

2. Rick shared a humorous yet sobering story about a rivalry he had with a pastor across town. God showed him that his attitude was blocking the revival he longed to experience. In what ways can you identify with Rick's situation? Is there someone you have been holding a grudge toward and even criticizing to others? Is it possible that some of your prayers have gone unanswered because of the hostility in your heart toward this person? What is the Lord showing you that you need to do to make things right?

Notes

CLAIM YOUR FREE RESOURCE!

As a way of introducing you further to the teaching ministry of Rick Renner, we would like to send you free of charge his teaching CD, "How To Receive a Miraculous Touch From God."

In His earthly ministry, Jesus commonly healed *all* who were sick of *all* their diseases. In this profound message, learn about the manifold dimensions of Christ's wisdom, goodness, power, and love toward all humanity who came to Him in faith with their needs.

☑ **YES, I want to receive Rick Renner's monthly teaching letter!**

Simply scan the QR code to claim this resource or go to: **renner.org/claim-your-free-offer**

WITH US!

 renner.org    facebook.com/rickrenner

 youtube.com/rennerministries    instagram.com/rickrrenner

www.ingramcontent.com/pod-product-compliance
Lightning Source LLC
Chambersburg PA
CBHW061259040426
42444CB00010B/2421